10 Reasons Black Americans Should Definitely Vote for Donald Trump

By Milton Chastain

TABLE OF CONTENTS

DEDICATION

This book is dedicated to the following individuals, and others, for the courage of their convictions:

Deneen Borelli

Mark Burns

Stacey Dash

Larry Elder

Hon. Minister Louis Farrakhan

Lynnette "Diamond" Hardaway and Rochelle "Silk" Richardson ('Stump for Trump' girls)

Omarosa Manigault

Steve Parson

Jamiel Shaw, Sr.

Thomas Milton Street, Sr.

And, of course, Donald Trump

INTRODUCTION

Introduction

In light of the harsh systemic and historic injustices blacks experience, it's worth it for black voters to consider Donald Trump's plan to provide black communities with opportunities for advancement.

Trump is one of the most successful business leaders in the world. His decision to enter the 2016 U.S. presidential race – without ever holding a seat in political office – surprised plenty of people. And over the years, his persona as a magnetic, entertaining – though often shrewd -- television personality influenced public opinion.

However, as millions of people listen to the presidential hopeful share his vision, passion and patriotism, he sparks the nation to remember we all want to make America great again.

He campaigns on a bold and common sense approach to economic reform, improvement in national security, strong international relations, and overall national well-being. In addition, he prides himself as an effective leader. "The thing that will surprise people, I'll be a unifier," Trump says. "I think I'll bring people together, and that includes blacks and whites and everything. I think people will come together."

Therefore, whether you're a voter looking at the field of options, or already a decided Trump supporter (and member of the "silent majority") -- this book offers insight into how Donald Trump is great for black people – and great for America.

1. "BLACK LIVES ARE VERY IMPORTANT, WHITE LIVES ARE VERY IMPORTANT, AND, TO ME, ALL LIVES ARE IMPORTANT, VERY, VERY IMPORTANT."

Trump Will Improve Blacks' Living Conditions

Donald Trump says, and will likely continue saying, incendiary remarks. And people are, rightfully so, quick to criticize his seemingly offensive comments, especially about minorities.

However, Trump also demonstrates significant efforts – beyond other candidates – to listen to and support minorities' needs.

For instance, he addressed the threat of police brutality against black Americans.

In July 2015, Anderson Cooper interviewed Trump to discuss Sandra Bland, a black woman stopped in Waller County, Texas, for what police described as a failure to signal a lane change.

After an argument between Bland and the officer, he removed her from her car and threatened he would "light her up." He brutally put her on the ground and arrested her. Then Bland was taken to a Waller County jail, where -- three days later -- she was found dead in her jail cell.

An autopsy determined her death was due to suicide, though her family and many activists questioned the determination.

Here is an excerpt from Cooper's interview:

Cooper: To African-Americans in this country, and there's a lot of people who believe they are treated differently by police, do you believe that there's a problem with that?

Trump: I hope not, but I will tell you that I saw that clip -- on your show, by the way. I thought it was terrible. He was so aggressive. It was a traffic signal, as I understand it. And, you know, who gets out of a car for a traffic signal? I haven't been pulled over in a while, actually. But, seriously he just looked very aggressive. I didn't like his demeanor. I thought it was terrible to be honest with you. And I'm a huge fan of the police. I think the police have to be given back power but this guy was overly aggressive, terribly aggressive.

Cooper: Do you think that happens to African-Americans more than it does to you or I?

Trump: I hope it doesn't, but it might. And, you know, I have a great relationship with African-Americans, as you possibly have heard. I just have great respect for them and, you know, they like me. I like them. The answer is, it possibly does. It shouldn't and it's very sad...I will say, though, in this case I watched that so closely. I watched it a few times. He was terrible.

In addition to being outspoken on police brutality, Trump's presidential campaign platform includes plans to improve black communities.

Trump's advisor, Michael Cohen, (as reported by Yahoo News reporter Hunter Walker) said Trump created a four-step plan to "help the African-American community."

"There are four things that are needed," Cohen said. "First... you've got to bring back God into the neighborhood. Number two, jobs. Three, tax incentives. You've got to create businesses in the neighborhood. And, four, education. And the education sort of mirrored, you know, with God because they say that the best education that you could ever get would be from your clergy."

To that point, in November 2015, Trump met with a group of black pastors. After the meeting, he said, "Black lives are very important, white lives are very important, and, to me, all lives are important, very, very important."

Trump's meeting included Omarosa Manigault, a black woman and former star on Trump's business competition show, *The Apprentice*. She is now an ordained minister in Los Angeles. After emerging from the pastors' meeting, Manigault announced,

"Donald Trump is committed to the black community."

Trump's willingness to speak out about issues affecting black Americans -- and partner with leaders and community members to identify solutions -- is both respectable and symbolic of a true American leader.

2. "I'm a Big, Big, Big Second Amendment Person! Big, Big!"

Trump Will Act Against Gun Violence

Black Americans experience gun violence at higher rates than other communities. According to the U.S. Department of Justice Bureau of Justice Statistics, from 1980 to 2008, blacks were disproportionately represented as both homicide victims and offenders.

The victimization rate for blacks (27.8 per 100,000) was six times higher than the rate for whites (4.5 per 100,000). The offending rate for blacks (34.4 per 100,000) was almost eight times higher than the rate for whites (4.5 per 100,000).

As Derryck Green wrote in a 2013 Western Journalism article, *The Real Truth About Blacks and Gun Violence,* "First, some of the cities with the harshest gun laws also have the highest rates of black-on-black gun violence. This is no coincidence. Second…America's children need to be protected from gun violence, but not necessarily with more gun laws. Restrictive gun laws punish only those who follow the law, not those who don't. This is precisely why we call lawbreakers criminals. No matter how many (more) laws are created with the intention of reducing gun violence, criminals, by definition, will disregard these laws, knowing that their potential victims will be increasingly defenseless."

As Trump's platform emphasizes, one of the main contributors to gun violence is the inability for law-abiding citizens to obtain guns for self-protection. "Study after study has shown that very few criminals are stupid enough to try and pass a background check – they get their guns from friends/family members or by stealing them," Trump says. "So the overwhelming majority of people who go through background checks are law-abiding gun owners."

Trump's plan to reduce gun violence includes the following:

- **Enforce The Laws On The Books:** "We need to get serious about prosecuting violent criminals. We need to bring back and expand programs like Project Exile and get gang members and drug dealers off the street. When we do, crime will go down and our cities and communities will be safer places to live," Trump says.

As Trump explains, "several years ago there was a tremendous program in Richmond, Virginia called Project Exile. It said that if a violent felon uses a gun to commit a crime, you will be prosecuted in federal court and go to prison for five years – no parole or early release. Obama's former Attorney General,

Eric Holder, called that a 'cookie cutter' program. That's ridiculous. I call that program a success. Murders committed with guns in Richmond decreased by over 60 percent when Project Exile was in place – in the first two years of the program alone, 350 armed felons were taken off the street...We need to bring back and expand programs like Project Exile and get gang members and drug dealers off the street. When we do, crime will go down and our cities and communities will be safer places to live."

Trump's plan to increase community safety includes the following:

- **Empower law-abiding gun owners to defend themselves:** "Law enforcement is great, they do a tremendous job, but they can't be everywhere all of the time. Our personal protection is ultimately up to us. That's why I'm a gun owner, that's why I have a concealed carry permit, and that's why tens of millions of Americans have concealed carry permits as well. It's just common sense. To make America great again, we're going to go after criminals and put the law back on the side of the law-abiding," Trump says.

- **Fix Our Broken Mental Health System:** "All of the tragic mass murders that occurred in the past several years have something in common – there were red flags that were ignored. We can't allow that to continue. We need to expand treatment programs, because most people with mental health problems aren't violent, they just need help. But for those who are violent, a danger to themselves or others, we need to get them off the street before they can terrorize our communities. This is just common sense," Trump says.

Toward defending the rights of law-abiding gun owners, Trump proposes, "law-abiding people should be allowed to own the firearm of their choice. The government has no business dictating what types of firearms good, honest people are allowed to own."

In addition, Trump says the national background check system for gun purchasers must be made more effective. "Too many states are failing to put criminal and mental health records into the system – and it should go without saying that a system's only going to be as effective as the records that are put into it. What we need to do is fix the system we have and make it work as intended. What we don't need to do is expand a broken system."

Lastly, toward improving the national background system, Trump proposes the implementation of a national right to carry. "The right of self-defense doesn't stop at the end of your driveway. That's why I have a concealed carry permit and why tens of millions of Americans do, too. That permit should be valid in all 50 states. A driver's license works in every state, so it's common sense that a concealed carry permit should work in every state. If we can do that for driving – which is a privilege, not a right – then surely we can do that for concealed carry, which is a right, not a privilege," Trump says.

In Trump's book, *The America We Deserve*, he wrote, "We can have safe streets. But unless we stand up for tough anticrime policies, they will be replaced by policies that emphasize criminals' rights over those of ordinary citizens. Soft criminal sentences are based on the proposition that criminals are the victims of society. A lot of people in high places really do believe that criminals are victims. The only victim of a violent crime is the person getting shot, stabbed, or raped. The perpetrator is never a victim. He's nothing more than a predator."

As a presidential candidate, Trump maintains his stance. "Violent crime in cities like Baltimore, Chicago and many others is out of control. Drug dealers and gang members are given a slap on the wrist and turned loose on the street. This needs to stop," he says.

At a rally in Manassas, Virginia in December 2015, black pastor, and former Pennsylvania state senator, Thomas Milton Street, Sr. said, "I want to address this issue of Black Lives Matter. Black lives matter, no matter who killed them, and there's been more people killed with black-on-black crime in America than there has been with white people killing. In Philadelphia, from 2007 to 2015, over 3,000 black people were shot dead by black people! And my question is, 'Where was 'Black Lives Matter?' They weren't around! My question is, will you come to Philadelphia and address the black community on what we're going to do about stopping the crime in the black community, and black-on-black crime in the black community, and crime in our schools? Will you do that?"

"The answer is yes," Trump said.

Trump understands that for the country to thrive, we require practical and effective gun rights' policies. He also understands that access to firearms plays a significant role in the safety of black neighborhoods. He will be a leader that looks at the facts and advocates accordingly for policy change.

3. "I Will Make Our Military So Strong and So Powerful, Nobody's Going to Mess With Us!"

Trump Will Improve National Security Measures

The United States has long prided itself as a nation with the best defense system in the world.

Now, because of devastating terrorist attacks by Islamic extremists, the U.S. and several other countries face a new, more complex threat – one that requires new military strategies.

The Institute for Economics & Peace reported in 2014 that, since 2000, there have been over 61,000 terrorist attacks, killing more than 140,000 people worldwide.

In addition, the Global Terrorism Index, based on the University of Maryland's database of terrorist attacks around the world since 1970, demonstrates that from 2013 to 2014, there was an 80 percent increase in terrorism-related fatalities – and 67 countries experienced at least one or more deaths from terrorism, as opposed to only 59 countries in 2013.

There are far too many examples of terrorist attacks – and there seems to be an even more devastating ripple effect that must be acknowledged.

As we're sadly aware, approximately 3,000 people were killed during the terrorist attacks of September 11, 2001. The Islamic extremist group al-Qaeda hijacked and flew planes into the Pentagon near Washington, D.C., a field in Pennsylvania and the World Trade Center in New York.

In November 2009, Nidal Hassan, a U.S. Army major and psychiatrist, shot and killed 13 people and injured 33 at Fort Hood military base in Texas. He declared his motivation was to defend the Taliban's leadership in Afghanistan.

Overall, there's a rise in terrorism by Islamic extremists, destroying lives and a sense of safety around the world.

Here are just a few more examples of such atrocities:

- In January 2015, Islamic extremists killed 17 people, including civilians and police, in France. Then, in November 2015, Islamic extremists coordinated terrorist attacks in France – including suicide bombings and mass shootings -- killing more than 130 and injuring over 350 people. (That attack is noted as the deadliest attack in France since World World II.) The Islamic State of Iraq and the Levant (ISIL) claimed responsibility as retaliation for France's airstrikes in Iraq and Syria.

- In December 2015, 14 people were killed and 22 were seriously injured in a terrorist attack carried out by a Islamic extremist married couple in San Bernardino, California.

- In January 2016, an al-Qaeda-linked terrorist group killed 29 people in Burkina Faso, resulting from an overtaking of a hotel commonly used by Western diplomats.

In addition, thousands of people are terrorized annually by Boko Haram, Nigeria's militant Islamist group. (The group is known for using bombings, assassinations and abductions toward their objective to overthrow the government and create an Islamic state.) According to a BBC article entitled, *Who are Nigeria's Boko Haram Islamists?*, Boko Haram "promotes a version of Islam which makes it "haram," or forbidden, for Muslims to take place in any political or social activity associated with Western society."

If ever there was a time to have a strong leader, one who will make decisions – possibly controversial, unpopular, ugly but necessary decisions – this is it.

In December 2015, Trump issued a statement on preventing Muslim immigration that read: "Donald J. Trump is calling for a total and complete shutdown of Muslims entering the United States until our country's representatives can figure out what is going on. Until we are able to determine and understand this problem and the dangerous threat it poses, our country cannot be the victims of horrendous attacks by people that believe only in Jihad, and have no sense of reason or respect for human life." (Initially, Trump's campaign indicated the plan meant Muslims American citizens would not be able to return to the U.S., though Trump later stated they would be permitted.)

On a *Morning Joe* interview the same month, Trump said, "We are at war with radical Islam. We have to get our hands around a very serious problem and it's getting worse. And you will have more World Trade Centers, and you will have more bigger than the World Trade Center, if you don't toughen up, smarten up, and use our heads."

Pastor Mark Burns, a black televangelist and co-founder of the NOW television network, supports Trump's stance.

"This, by any means, is not an attack on the Islamic faith, especially the Muslim-Americans or the black Muslim-Americans here in the United States of America. This is simply an opportunity, a chance to weed out those who are abroad, who are immigrants," Burns said. "Not Muslim-Americans, but immigrants that have infiltrated using the Islamic faith to infiltrate the United States of America and to … cause damage, you know, using the Sharia law here in America, create terrorism."

Here's what the Honorable Minister Louis Farrakhan of the Nation of Islam said in an interview with Alex Jones in January 2016:

"Our government has gone into nations with money from our Congress to stimulate the dissatisfied and then arm them against a government that is their government. That's what America did in Libya, that's what they're doing in Syria, and the blowback now is they have created a refugee crisis that is destabilizing the countries in Europe.

So when Mr. Trump said we can't allow these Muslims, refugees into America, now, a lot of people were upset with him, but I know, sir, that the hatred for America in the Muslim world is building.

As we told Mr. Bush, no Muslim leader could call for Jihad and have it stick. No Muslim leader had the power to unite the whole Muslim world, I said. But America's policies will unite those people against the West, and it is happening.

So, in this way, Mr. Trump, I think, is wise to vet anyone coming from that area into America because the hatred for America is in the streets now. So if those people are refugees and America feels 'I gotta let 10,000 of them in because America created the problem,' now, if you let them in and you don't vet them carefully, you might be letting in your own destruction."

Trump's patriotism is undeniable.

"I feel I have a great obligation to the country and I think I'm saying something that has to be said," Trump said. "I would have had bin Laden knocked out and maybe the World Trade Center, as it was, would be standing right now."

Regarding an international force against ISIS, Trump said, "I'd knock out the capital, and I'd knock it out big and strong. I'd take over the oil and I'd keep the oil. You'll need some ground troops...We're going to take the oil. We're going to give some of the profits of the oil to our Wounded Warriors, and to our veterans, and to the families whose sons and daughters died in Iraq, Afghanistan, and Syria." He added, "You gotta take them out swifty and strongly...I would bomb wherever they are. Right now, we're being so politically correct. Nice and gentle, nice and gentle. We've got a cancer there and the cancer is ISIS. Life means nothing to them."

Lastly, when asked if Trump would support having 10,000 ground troops sent to defeat ISIS, he said, "I would."

The United States may not want to admit it's at war – but it certainly is – and several dangerous ideological groups are certainly at war with the U.S. Trump acknowledges that what the U.S. has done, so far, in response to terrorism has not been enough. We haven't stopped the terrorists. We haven't prevented them from destroying America bit by bit. And while Trump may not be able to prevent every terrorist attack – no one person could -- he will give everything possible to keep America safe, by any means necessary.

4. "I'm Fighting for The Vets."

Trump Respects Soldiers

Trump aims to implement a plan that will honor the service of millions of veterans. And blacks, in particular, have contributed monumentally to the historic success of the U.S. military.

About 350,000 blacks served overseas in France during World War I. Thousands also served in World War II, including a number of black women who joined the new women's auxiliaries. (The prestigious Tuskegee Airmen, known for their red-tailed P-51 Mustang fighters, never lost an escorted plane during World War II, as they carried out hundreds of escort missions.)

Blacks served in many more military operations, including the Vietnam War (1959-1973) and comprised 22 percent of the total Army serving during the Persian Gulf War of the early 1990s, during which Colin Powell was the Chairman of the Joint Chiefs of Staff during Operation Desert Storm.

In 2003, there were approximately 254,000 blacks serving the Army as an Active-Duty, Reserves or National Guard soldier, or as an Army Civilian, as reported by the U.S. Office of Army Demographics.

As of 2012, the U.S. military was comprised of 16.4 percent blacks. And according to the U.S. Census Bureau, in 2013, there were approximately 2.2 million black veterans in the U.S.

Trump's Veterans Plan includes expediting the receipt of medical care needed by veterans, with a strategy to "decrease wait times, improve healthcare outcomes, and facilitate a seamless transition from service into civilian life."

The Trump Plan will "support the whole veteran...addressing their invisible wounds, investing in our service members' post-active duty success, transforming the VA to meet the needs of 21st century service members, and better meeting the needs of our female veterans."

Trump will also increase funding for post-traumatic stress disorder (PTSD), traumatic brain injury and suicide prevention services, increase funding for job training and placement services, and expand VA services for female veterans.

One key plan, according to Trump's agenda is that "exposing and addressing the VA's inefficiencies and shortcomings will be rewarded, not punished."

With the threat of full-out wars looming – especially in response to ever-growing terrorist threats -- there's a subsequent likelihood that more Americans, including black Americans will serve in the armed forces. With this in mind, Trump's plan will provide as much a safety net as possible so that when veterans need assistance and care, their needs will be met.

5. "WE HAVE TO BRING OUR COUNTRY BACK"

Trump Puts American Citizens First

Trump insists Americans deserve jobs and economic opportunities ahead of illegal immigrants.

In Trump's detailed immigration plan, he says "U.S. taxpayers have been asked to pick up hundreds of billions in healthcare costs, housing costs, education costs, welfare costs, etc. Indeed, the annual cost of free tax credits alone paid to illegal immigrants quadrupled to $4.5 billion in 2011. The effects on jobseekers have also been disastrous, and black Americans have been particularly harmed."

And he's not alone in his stance.

"Trump's plan would help black Americans," Deneen Borelli, a black conservative, political news contributor and author of *Blacklash: How Obama and the Left are Driving Americans to the Government Plantation* said on "Hannity" in August 2015. "When you look at this wave of illegal immigrants who would be coming into the country, they're competing for the same low-skilled jobs. It's driving down wages."

Larry Elder, a black lawyer, writer, television and radio personality, especially on political issues, said, "Coretta Scott King wrote a letter about 25 years ago to Congress and urged them not to lighten up sanctions against employers who knowingly hire illegal aliens because they threaten jobs for black people. Donald Trump is the only one talking about it -- to a lesser extent, maybe Dr. Ben Carson is. That is why Trump is making in-roads and may even crack that 95 percent, monolithic, democratic black vote."

Understandably, critically discussing illegal immigrants is often viewed as insensitive. However, it's a necessary discussion.

"We have a country, you need borders and you need laws," Trump says.

Jamiel Shaw, Sr. agrees.

"In March the 2nd, 2008 my son was shot dead in the street like a dog by an illegal alien gang banger, 18th street gang banger," Shaw said. "He was on his third gun charge. Now we hear all these gun people talking about banning guns, but you have an illegal alien on his third gun charge, never been deported. And the guy shot him through his hand into his head and killed him. It was vicious."

Shaw decided to endorse Trump due to his family's tragic circumstance.

"That's why we need Donald Trump because Donald Trump is going to make it safe again," Shaw said. "Trump is the only person that reached out to me, out of all the politicians, all the black politicians in L.A. Nobody cares, it's all about illegal aliens! That's all they care about, they don't care about us as Americans! Trump wants to make America first, okay! We need that! Our kids, all of our kids, deserve to grow up."

He continued, "Why do we have to be under this oppression from illegal aliens, and they're getting the American dream and we're getting the American nightmare? You know, it's not fair, and the only way we can fix it is with Donald Trump. I don't see no other way, if it was there it would have happened. Before Trump, it was nothing going on. Now that he's here, they're scared and we have to make sure it happens because it's going to protect all of us and make us safe. And we've got to stand with Trump and you have to trust him the way I do. Because I believe that he was sent from God."

On *Fox & Friends*, Shaw explained to Tucker Carlson, "There's thousands of people who've been murdered by illegal aliens…When people hear the stories, they'll stand up, and they want something done about it." He added, "When you speak up they call you a racist and things like that. They call me racist, but I doesn't care. I ask people all the time, 'What would you do if someone, anybody murdered your loved one, especially an illegal alien?' See they can't answer that question truthfully."

Trump cites a 2011 U.S. Government Accountability Office study that found U.S. prisons consisted of 351,000 criminal aliens who committed crimes after illegally entering America. "The GAO says that the annual price tag to incarcerate these thugs is $1.1 billion. And get this: criminal aliens have an average of seven arrests."

As one solution, Trump wants to construct a more effective barrier between the U.S. and Mexico – designed to lead to increased safety for Americans.

"I would build a wall between our country and Mexico because people come from all over the world. I encourage legal citizenship," Trump said in July 2015. "But what I don't encourage is people coming into our country illegally, and I don't encourage where a government forces some people in, that the government doesn't want. And these people reap havoc on our population."

Ultimately, Trump's plan to better regulate who enters the country will allow for more focus on ensuring Americans have access to necessary resources.

6. "PART OF THE BEAUTY OF ME IS THAT I'M VERY RICH"

Trump's Got His Own Money

Trump's socioeconomic status is important because his wealth allows him a certain amount of freedom to speak on the issues that matter most to the American people, not to just lobbyists and special interest groups. Furthermore, he can act on creating policies that will directly provide a benefit to the American people.

In December 2015, on *LIVE with Kelly and Michael*, Trump explained his financial self-reliance and how his economic status plays into his presidential campaign.

"People really like the fact I'm the only person -- out of everybody -- Democrat, Republican -- that's self-funding," Trump said. "I'm putting up my own money, and so far I haven't had to spend that much because I haven't done any commercials of note. I've done virtually no commercials, and I see a couple of people are up to $34, $35 million. One's at $48 million, and I'm at, like, nothing, it's embarrassing. But I get so much television...but I'm self-funding my campaign.

And I'll tell you something, people love that I'm self-funding because, you know, I play the game as well as anybody's ever played it. I know politicians, I've dealt, and when you give somebody a million, $2 million, $5 million to run -- that's your person. And if you have a company or if you have a country that you're a representative, as a lobbyist or something, representing China or one of these countries that are ripping us off, and they're giving a lot of money to the candidates, believe me, those candidates are absolutely in the bag. And they will sell out the folks, they will sell out our country, in order to take care of their donors. And, I mean, who understands that better than I do?

So the fact that I'm the only self-funder, I put up all my own money and, you know what, people love it. I think it's one of the reasons I'm leading by so much, because I can't be bought."

Furthermore, Trump demonstrates in-depth knowledge of the American economy.

"Why are we footing the bill and getting nothing in return?," he said. "I'll give you the answer. It's because our so-called leaders in Washington know absolutely nothing about negotiations and deal making."

"Imagine how much money the average American would save if we busted the OPEC cartel. Imagine how much stronger economic shape we would be in if we made the Iraqi government agree to a cost-sharing plan that paid us back the $1.5 trillion we've dropped on liberating Iraq," he said.

Trump also proposes making changes with how the United States does business with China.

He says that, according to a study by the Peterson Institute for International Economics, even a 20 percent revaluation of Chinese currency would create 300,000 to 700,000 American jobs.

"Getting China to stop playing its currency charades can begin whenever we elect a president ready to take decisive action," Trump says. "It's the utter weakness and failure to fight for American interests from Geithner and Obama that have left us underwriting China's economic rise and our own economic collapse. It's a plain fact: free trade requires having fair rules that apply to everyone."

All in all, Trump bankrolls his own campaign and he understands the economy better than most politicians. His leadership would lead the nation to become a stronger global economic power.

7. "I'm a Rich Guy, But I Have this Great Relationship With the Working People of this Country"

Trump Will Alleviate the Financial Struggle

Trump understands the importance of financial reform to improve conditions for struggling Americans.

In 2013, the annual median income of black households was around $34,598 compared with the nation at $51,939. The same year, the poverty rate for blacks was 27.2 percent, while nationally it was 14.5 percent.

Trump has a plan to improve financial conditions, especially for low-income Americans. One part of his plan is to improve the effectiveness of welfare-to-work programs.

In Trump's book, *Time to Get Tough*, he writes, "The secret to the 1996 Welfare Reform Act's success was that it tied welfare to work. To get your check, you had to prove that you were enrolled in job-training or trying to find work. But here's the rub: the 1996 Welfare Reform Act only dealt with one program, Aid to Families with Dependent Children (AFDC), not the other seventy-six welfare programs which, today, cost taxpayers more than

$900 billion annually. We need to take a page from the 1996 reform and do the same for other welfare programs. Benefits should have strings attached to them. After all, if it's our money recipients are getting, we the people should have a say in how it's spent."

Trump says the American work ethic will lead Americans to prosperity.

"That's what I find so morally offensive about welfare dependency: it robs people of the chance to improve. Work gives every day a sense of purpose. A job well done provides a sense of pride and accomplishment. I love to work. In fact, I like working so much that I seldom take vacations.

Because I work so hard, I've been privileged to create jobs for tens of thousands of people. And on my hit show *The Apprentice*, I get to work with people from all walks of life. I'm known for my famous line, 'You're fired!', but the truth is, I don't like firing people. Sometimes you have to do it, but it's never fun or easy. One of my favorite parts of business is seeing how work transforms people into better, more confident, more competent individuals. It's inspiring and beautiful to watch."

During a December 2015 rally in Las Vegas, Trump also spoke about his plan regarding the healthcare system. "We will repeal, we will replace Obamacare. It's dying away. In [20]17, it's dead. It's all the wrong people joining, the wrong income," Trump said. "It is a mess like nobody's ever seen. It's dying. We're losing our doctors. You know the insurance companies make a fortune, they took good care of Obama. They're the big beneficiaries. We're going to get rid of the artificial borders. We're going to have real bidding. We're going to have great insurance, it's going to be less money, and it's going to be good. Your premiums are going up, right now, 25, 35, 45 and 55 percent. Your deductibles are through the roof, you'll never even get to use it unless you're dead. You won't get to use it, and it's a disgrace that is was ever approved in the first place."

Trump also proposes a new tax plan to help Americans keep more of their wealth. Here's a brief summary:

First, he says the U.S. must eliminate the death tax. Second, he wants to ensure businesses' tax rates go no higher than 15 percent. To this point, he says, "Capitalism requires capital. When government robs capital from investors, it takes away the money that creates jobs."

Third, anyone earning under $25,000 annually would owe no income tax. (Married couples earning under $50,000 would also owe nothing in income taxes.) Lastly, the tax code would be reduced from seven levels to four levels ranging from 0-25 percent.

As he writes on his website, donaldjtrump.com, "This plan also reduces or eliminates loopholes used by the very rich and special interests made unnecessary or redundant by the new lower tax rates on individuals and companies."

He continues, "When the income tax was first introduced, just one percent of Americans had to pay it. It was never intended as a tax most Americans would pay. The Trump plan eliminates the income tax for over 73 million households. Forty-two million households that currently file complex forms to determine they don't owe any income taxes will now file a one page form saving them time, stress, uncertainty and an average of $110 in preparation costs. Over 31 million households get the same simplification and keep on average nearly $1,000 of their hard-earned money."

Trump knows the required tax rates and adjustments needed to improve financial conditions for all Americans. And black Americans have, perhaps, the most to gain by supporting Trump's plans to improve the economy.

8. "I WILL BE THE GREATEST JOBS PRESIDENT THAT GOD EVER CREATED."

Trump's an Employer

According to the 2014 Census Bureau, blacks comprised 13.2 percent of the U.S. population – but a disproportionately high segment of unemployed Americans.

"The black community is still number one in poverty. We're the poorest community in the country," Steve Parson, a conservative black pastor said in 2015. "The black American is the poorest ethic race in America, so we want a change, and not the kind of change that Obama was talking about. I'm talking about a change where we start, for poverty, we start receiving wealth. For lack, we start receiving and getting an abundance. I believe the key to that is the entrepreneur spirit and I believe Donald Trump is going to come in here with an entrepreneur spirit and he's going to make more people wealthier."

And, as Trump pointed out during a November 2015 Republican debate, "over the years, I've created tens of thousands of jobs and a great company. It's a company I'm very proud of. Some of the most iconic assets anywhere in the world."

Trump knows tough decisions are necessary. "I'm going to bring jobs back," he says. "I'm going to bring jobs back from China, from Japan, from all of these places, including Mexico, by the way, which is really taking advantage of the United States both on the border and from the standpoint of trade. So, I'll be bringing jobs back...nobody else can do it like me."

Parson says Trump will be good for the inner city communities, too, "by teaching, encouraging, backing those of us that are wanting to educate our people to be business owners. You see, you give a man a fish, you only feed him for a day. But if you can teach that man to fish, you feed him for a lifetime. So we just believe that Donald Trump is the man that can do it."

"We here in Virginia, we're in the process of putting together a coalition of black ministers and black pastors, and we plan on meeting with him and seeing if we can help him with his economic plan for the inner city. He mentioned about bringing manufacturers back to the country, giving them incentives for wanting to bring their businesses here," Parson said. "We're going to talk to him about bringing these manufacturing companies around the inner city, not in the inner city, but in some of the areas around the inner cities that will allow people who are less educated and don't have the work experience to work in these plants and factories and generate good income."

After attending a meeting with Trump and black pastors, Parson said, "This meeting was extremely successful. There was extremely strong support. He received many, many endorsements from the pastors that were there. It was a jam-packed room, standing support for Mr. Trump. Very good dialogue that we had back and forth and Donald Trump made it very clear that he's willing to do whatever it takes to win the black vote."

Trump says nearly 40 percent of black teenagers are unemployed. And he says part of the issue is immigrant workers presenting challenges for poor and working class Americans who want to get ahead.

"We need to control the admission of new low-earning workers in order to: help wages grow, get teenagers back to work, aid minorities' rise into the middle class, help schools and communities falling behind, and to ensure our immigrant members of the national family become part of the American dream," Trump says.

Trump's plan emphasizes a "requirement to hire American workers first. Too many visas, like the H-1B, have no such requirement. In the year 2015, with 92 million Americans outside the workforce and incomes collapsing, we need companies to hire from the domestic pool of unemployed. Petitions for workers should be mailed to the unemployment office, not USCIS."

He adds, "Raising the prevailing wage paid to H-1Bs will force companies to give these coveted entry-level jobs to the existing domestic pool of unemployed native and immigrant workers in the U.S., instead of flying in cheaper workers from overseas. This will improve the number of black, Hispanic and female workers in Silicon Valley who have been passed over in favor of the H-1B program."

Trump also wants to increase job programs for inner city youth. "The J-1 visa jobs program for foreign youth will be terminated and replaced with a resume bank for inner city youth provided to all corporate subscribers to the J-1 visa program," he says.

Overall, Trump is already a job creator and he could create even more jobs for American citizens through his reform plans. He prioritizes Americans as being the most deserving of employment opportunities and he has a plan to ensure more Americans receive the advantage toward reaching these opportunities.

9. "There's Going to Be Change -- But Real Change, Not Obama Change"

Trump's A Unifier

"Many of us really feel that this is a season and a time for a strong leader that can really bring Americans together," Pastor Mark Burns said leading up to Trump's meeting with black preachers in New York in December 2015. "There are no Judas's, there are no Uncle Tom's, there are no coons that are selling out the black race like many have stated, just for some 30 pieces of silver. Those of us who are there have met the man, and fallen in love with the character of Donald Trump."

He's certainly not the only one who speaks adoringly of Trump.

The 'Stump for Trump' girls -- two black women, sisters and web-famous Trump supporters -- changed their party affiliation from Democrat to Republican in September 2015. (Their names are Lynnette "Diamond" Hardaway and Rochelle "Silk" Richardson.)

Here's an interview they did with CNN's Don Lemon in August 2015.

"When I looked at him and I looked at his ideals, and he was talking my language, pretty much, I said, 'Oh, my God! This is going to be our next president, right here!,'" Richardson said. "And I just felt it! I knew it, he resonated so well with me."

"He said he was going to secure that border, and then he's going to bring jobs back to Americans. So that means that Americans not only are going to be surviving, they're going to be able to thrive in this country. And that's what I love," Hardaway said. "He is going to make America great again! You hear me! He is going to make America great and that's why I stump for the Trump! We have too many things happening in our country! We have a border that needs to be secure! We have ISIS trying to cut off heads! We have people going into movie theaters shooting it up, Don! We've got to secure this border! We got to make America great again! We got to make America great again and the only way we can do that, baby, is with Donald Trump!"

In an interview with CNN's Jake Tapper in October 2015, Trump said, "I'm going to unify the country. Over the years, I've gotten along with Democrats and I've gotten along with Republicans...I get along with everybody. I will be a great unifier for our country."

Passion and support for Trump's policy plans emerge as Americans realize that a vote for him just makes sense for the country. He shines a light on important issues and offers an aggressive plan to restore the patriotic ideals Americans value most.

10. "Our Country Has to Win."

Trump's a Champion

After all the debates and rallies, petitions and protests, Tweets and news soundbites -- what's most important is that the U.S. emerges with a leader willing to do what's necessary to keep the country thriving and safe. And many agree that Trump is the best candidate to do so.

Stacey Dash, a black actress, television news personality, and author of *There Goes My Social Life: From Clueless to Conservative*, spoke on the Fox News show "Outnumbered" in support of Donald Trump.

"Understand that he wants to make America great," Dash said. "Whatever it takes to do that, he wants to do that! And he's the man to do that. He's the man with the Rolodex to do that. He's the man with the power to do that, and he's the man who knows how to make deals! So he's the man to get people to cross the aisle and close the deals!"

Burns also expressed his Trump support to MSNBC's Kate Snow. "Trust me when I tell you, I'm not an Uncle Tom, no coon, nobody's been paid. I have not been offered a position. This is me looking at the politics and looking at an individual, a strong leader that I believe that's going to bridge and bring a strength back to America."

And, in December 2015, Parson announced, "I'm fully, 100 percent endorsing Donald Trump to be the next president of the United States. I believe he's best for America. I believe that he has a heart for people. And he's strong, and America needs to show some strength right now. And at the same time with him working with us, and we're working with him, I believe that he's going to direct capital toward the inner city. We're going to see prosperity, we're going to see jobs, we're going to see an end of unemployment crisis in America, and I'm just encouraging the black Americans, especially. Because, already there's a move of God. There's more people that are saying, 'I'm voting for Donald Trump. I'm not voting for the Republican, but I'm going to vote for Donald Trump.'"

Parson continued: "I just have a heart for people. I have a heart for my community. I have a heart for America -- and so does Donald Trump! He doesn't need to be president, he wants to be because he believes that he can help, and make America great again! He's got a passion, I actually say it's a calling and an anointing. Again, don't believe the lies; all those lies about him being a racist is coming from the Democratic, liberal media that is trying to keep him from being president. It's all political stuff, y'all! Listen, don't believe all that stuff! If you're going to believe anybody, believe a minister that's telling you that we're in store for the greatest financial move! We're in store for a wealth transfer! We're in store for a moving back to God that we've never seen before! Isn't it time! I believe it's our time, and it's our season, and, bless God, we're going to give God all the glory for it! Vote Donald Trump!"

--

Trump's candidacy speech says much of what he wants to do for the nation. It's included here for your enjoyment and additional clarity on where he stands:

Trump's Candidacy Speech (June 16, 2015):

So nice, thank you very much. That's really nice. Thank you. It's great to be at Trump Tower. It's great to be in a wonderful city, New York. And it's an honor to have everybody here. This is beyond anybody's expectations. There's been no crowd like this.

And, I can tell, some of the candidates, they went in. They didn't know the air-conditioner didn't work. They sweated like dogs.

They didn't know the room was too big, because they didn't have anybody there. How are they going to beat ISIS? I don't think it's gonna happen.

Our country is in serious trouble. We don't have victories anymore. We used to have victories, but we don't have them. When was the last time anybody saw us beating, let's say, China in a trade deal? They kill us. I beat China all the time. All the time.

When did we beat Japan at anything? They send their cars over by the millions, and what do we do? When was the last time you saw a Chevrolet in Tokyo? It doesn't exist, folks. They beat us all the time.

When do we beat Mexico at the border? They're laughing at us, at our stupidity. And now they are beating us economically. They are not our friend, believe me. But they're killing us economically.

The U.S. has become a dumping ground for everybody else's problems.

Thank you. It's true, and these are the best and the finest. When Mexico sends its people, they're not sending their best. They're not sending you. They're not sending you. They're sending people that have lots of problems, and they're bringing those problems with us. They're bringing drugs. They're bringing crime. They're rapists. And some, I assume, are good people.

But I speak to border guards and they tell us what we're getting. And it only makes common sense. It only makes common sense. They're sending us not the right people.

It's coming from more than Mexico. It's coming from all over South and Latin America, and it's coming probably— probably— from the Middle East. But we don't know. Because we have no protection and we have no competence, we don't know what's happening. And it's got to stop and it's got to stop fast.

Islamic terrorism is eating up large portions of the Middle East. They've become rich. I'm in competition with them.

They just built a hotel in Syria. Can you believe this? They built a hotel. When I have to build a hotel, I pay interest. They don't have to pay interest, because they took the oil that, when we left Iraq, I said we should've taken.

So now ISIS has the oil, and what they don't have, Iran has. And in 19— and I will tell you this, and I said it very strongly, years ago, I said— and I love the military, and I want to have the strongest military that we've ever had, and we need it more now than ever. But I said, "Don't hit Iraq," because you're going to totally destabilize the Middle East. Iran is going to take over the Middle East, Iran and somebody else will get the oil, and it turned out that Iran is now taking over Iraq. Think of it. Iran is taking over Iraq, and they're taking it over big league.

We spent $2 trillion in Iraq, $2 trillion. We lost thousands of lives, thousands in Iraq. We have wounded soldiers, who I love, I love — they're great — all over the place, thousands and thousands of wounded soldiers.

And we have nothing. We can't even go there. We have nothing. And every time we give Iraq equipment, the first time a bullet goes off in the air, they leave it.

Last week, I read 2,300 Humvees— these are big vehicles— were left behind for the enemy. 2,000? You would say maybe two, maybe four? 2,300 sophisticated vehicles, they ran, and the enemy took them.

Last quarter, it was just announced our gross domestic product— a sign of strength, right? But not for us. It was below zero. Whoever heard of this? It's never below zero.

Our labor participation rate was the worst since 1978. But think of it, GDP below zero, horrible labor participation rate.

And our real unemployment is anywhere from 18 to 20 percent. Don't believe the 5.6. Don't believe it.

That's right. A lot of people up there can't get jobs. They can't get jobs, because there are no jobs, because China has our jobs and Mexico has our jobs. They all have jobs.

But the real number, the real number is anywhere from 18 to 19 and maybe even 21 percent, and nobody talks about it, because it's a statistic that's full of nonsense.

Our enemies are getting stronger and stronger by the way, and we as a country are getting weaker. Even our nuclear arsenal doesn't work.

It came out recently they have equipment that is 30 years old. They don't know if it worked. And I thought it was horrible when it was broadcast on television, because boy, does that send signals to Putin and all of the other people that look at us and they say, "That is a group of people, and that is a nation that truly has no clue. They don't know what they're doing. They don't know what they're doing."

We have a disaster called the big lie: Obamacare. Obamacare.

Yesterday, it came out that costs are going for people up 29, 39, 49, and even 55 percent, and deductibles are through the roof. You have to be hit by a tractor, literally, a tractor, to use it, because the deductibles are so high, it's virtually useless. It's virtually useless. It is a disaster.

And remember the $5 billion website? Five billion dollars we spent on a website, and to this day it doesn't work. A $5 billion website.

I have so many websites, I have them all over the place. I hire people, they do a website. It costs me $3. Five billion dollar website.

Well, you need somebody, because politicians are all talk, no action. Nothing's gonna get done. They will not bring us— believe me— to the promised land. They will not.

As an example, I've been on the circuit making speeches, and I hear my fellow Republicans. And they're wonderful people. I like them. They all want me to support them. They don't know how to bring it about. They come up to my office. I'm meeting with three of them in the next week. And they don't know— "Are you running? Are you not running? Could we have your support? What do we do? How do we do it?"

I like them. And I hear their speeches. And they don't talk jobs and they don't talk China. When was the last time you heard China is killing us? They're devaluing their currency to a level that you wouldn't believe. It makes it impossible for our companies to compete, impossible. They're killing us.

But you don't hear that from anybody else. You don't hear it from anybody else. And I watch the speeches.

I watch the speeches of these people, and they say the sun will rise, the moon will set, all sorts of wonderful things will happen. And people are saying,

"What's going on? I just want a job. Just get me a job. I don't need the rhetoric. I want a job."

And that's what's happening. And it's going to get worse, because remember, Obamacare really kicks in in '16, 2016. Obama is going to be out playing golf. He might be on one of my courses. I would invite him, I actually would say. I have the best courses in the world, so I'd say, you what, if he wants to— I have one right next to the White House, right on the Potomac. If he'd like to play, that's fine.

In fact, I'd love him to leave early and play, that would be a very good thing.

But Obamacare kicks in in 2016. Really big league. It is going to be amazingly destructive. Doctors are quitting. I have a friend who's a doctor, and he said to me the other day, "Donald, I never saw anything like it. I have more accountants than I have nurses. It's a disaster. My patients are beside themselves. They had a plan that was good. They have no plan now."

We have to repeal Obamacare, and it can be— and— and it can be replaced with something much better for everybody. Let it be for everybody. But much better and much less expensive for people and for the government. And we can do it.

So I've watched the politicians. I've dealt with them all my life. If you can't make a good deal with a politician, then there's something wrong with you.

You're certainly not very good. And that's what we have representing us. They will never make America great again. They don't even have a chance. They're controlled fully— they're controlled fully by the lobbyists, by the donors, and by the special interests, fully.

Yes, they control them. Hey, I have lobbyists. I have to tell you. I have lobbyists that can produce anything for me. They're great. But you know what? it won't happen. It won't happen. Because we have to stop doing things for some people, but for this country, it's destroying our country. We have to stop, and it has to stop now.

Now, our country needs— our country needs a truly great leader, and we need a truly great leader now. We need a leader that wrote "The Art of the Deal."

We need a leader that can bring back our jobs, can bring back our manufacturing, can bring back our military, can take care of our vets. Our vets have been abandoned.

And we also need a cheerleader.

You know, when President Obama was elected, I said, "Well, the one thing, I think he'll do well. I think he'll be a great cheerleader for the country. I think he'd be a great spirit."

He was vibrant. He was young. I really thought that he would be a great cheerleader.

He's not a leader. That's true. You're right about that.

But he wasn't a cheerleader. He's actually a negative force. He's been a negative force. He wasn't a cheerleader; he was the opposite.

We need somebody that can take the brand of the United States and make it great again. It's not great again.

We need — we need somebody — we need somebody that literally will take this country and make it great again. We can do that.

And, I will tell you, I love my life. I have a wonderful family. They're saying, "Dad, you're going to do something that's going to be so tough."

You know, all of my life, I've heard that a truly successful person, a really, really successful person and even modestly successful cannot run for public office. Just can't happen. And yet that's the kind of mindset that you need to make this country great again.

So ladies and gentlemen…I am officially running… for president of the United States, and we are going to make our country great again.

It can happen. Our country has tremendous potential. We have tremendous people.

We have people that aren't working. We have people that have no incentive to work. But they're going to have incentive to work, because the greatest social program is a job. And they'll be proud, and they'll love it, and they'll make much more than they would've ever made, and they'll be— they'll be doing so well, and we're going to be thriving as a country, thriving. It can happen.

I will be the greatest jobs president that God ever created. I tell you that.

I'll bring back our jobs from China, from Mexico, from Japan, from so many places. I'll bring back our jobs, and I'll bring back our money.

Right now, think of this: We owe China $1.3 trillion. We owe Japan more than that. So they come in, they take our jobs, they take our money, and then they loan us back the money, and we pay them in interest, and then the dollar goes up so their deal's even better.

How stupid are our leaders? How stupid are these politicians to allow this to happen? How stupid are they?

I'm going to tell you— thank you. I'm going to tell you a couple of stories about trade, because I'm totally against the trade bill for a number of reasons.

Number one, the people negotiating don't have a clue. Our president doesn't have a clue. He's a bad negotiator.

He's the one that did Bergdahl. We get Bergdahl, they get five killer terrorists that everybody wanted over there.

We get Bergdahl. We get a traitor. We get a no-good traitor, and they get the five people that they wanted for years, and those people are now back on the battlefield trying to kill us. That's the negotiator we have.

Take a look at the deal he's making with Iran. He makes that deal, Israel maybe won't exist very long. It's a disaster, and we have to protect Israel. But...

So we need people — I'm a free trader. But the problem with free trade is you need really talented people to negotiate for you. If you don't have talented people, if you don't have great leadership, if you don't have people that know business, not just a political hack that got the job because he made a contribution to a campaign, which is the way all jobs, just about, are gotten, free trade terrible.

Free trade can be wonderful if you have smart people, but we have people that are stupid. We have people that aren't smart. And we have people that are controlled by special interests. And it's just not going to work.

So, here's a couple of stories happened recently. A friend of mine is a great manufacturer. And, you know, China comes over and they dump all their stuff, and I buy it. I buy it, because, frankly, I have an obligation to buy it, because they devalue their currency so brilliantly, they just did it recently, and nobody thought they could do it again.

But with all our problems with Russia, with all our problems with everything — everything, they got away with it again. And it's impossible for our people here to compete.

So I want to tell you this story. A friend of mine who's a great manufacturer, calls me up a few weeks ago. He's very upset. I said, "What's your problem?"

He said, "You know, I make great product."

And I said, "I know. I know that because I buy the product."

He said, "I can't get it into China. They won't accept it. I sent a boat over and they actually sent it back. They talked about environmental, they talked about all sorts of crap that had nothing to do with it."

I said, "Oh, wait a minute, that's terrible. Does anyone know this?"

He said, "Yeah, they do it all the time with other people."

I said, "They send it back?"

"Yeah. So I finally got it over there and they charged me a big tariff. They're not supposed to be doing that. I told them."

Now, they do charge you tariff on trucks, when we send trucks and other things over there.

Ask Boeing. They wanted Boeing's secrets. They wanted their patents and all their secrets before they agreed to buy planes from Boeing.

Hey, I'm not saying they're stupid. I like China. I sell apartments for — I just sold an apartment for $15 million to somebody from China. Am I supposed to dislike them? I own a big chunk of the Bank of America Building at 1290 Avenue of the Americas, that I got from China in a war. Very valuable.

I love China. The biggest bank in the world is from China. You know where their United States headquarters is located? In this building, in Trump Tower. I love China. People say, "Oh, you don't like China?"

No, I love them. But their leaders are much smarter than our leaders, and we can't sustain our self with that. There's too much— it's like— it's like take the New England Patriots and Tom Brady and have them play your high school football team.

That's the difference between China's leaders and our leaders.

They are ripping us. We are rebuilding China. We're rebuilding many countries. China, you go there now, roads, bridges, schools, you never saw anything like it. They have bridges that make the George Washington Bridge look like small potatoes. And they're all over the place.

We have all the cards, but we don't know how to use them. We don't even know that we have the cards, because our leaders don't understand the game. We could turn off that spigot by charging them tax until they behave properly.

Now they're going militarily. They're building a military island in the middle of the South China sea. A military island. Now, our country could never do that because we'd have to get environmental clearance, and the environmentalist wouldn't let our country— we would never build in an ocean. They built it in about one year, this massive military port.

They're building up their military to a point that is very scary. You have a problem with ISIS. You have a bigger problem with China.

And, in my opinion, the new China, believe it or not, in terms of trade, is Mexico.

So this man tells me about the manufacturing. I say, "That's a terrible story. I hate to hear it."

But I have another one, Ford.

So Mexico takes a company, a car company that was going to build in Tennessee, rips it out. Everybody thought the deal was dead. Reported it in the Wall Street Journal recently. Everybody thought it was a done deal. It's going in and that's going to be it, going into Tennessee. Great state, great people.

All of a sudden, at the last moment, this big car manufacturer, foreign, announces they're not going to Tennessee. They're gonna spend their $1 billion in Mexico instead. Not good.

Now, Ford announces a few weeks ago that Ford is going to build a $2.5 billion car and truck and parts manufacturing plant in Mexico. Two point five billion dollars, it's going to be one of the largest in the world. Ford. Good company.

So I announced that I'm running for president. I would...

... one of the early things I would do, probably before I even got in— and I wouldn't even use— you know, I have— I know the smartest negotiators in the world. I know the good ones. I know the bad ones. I know the overrated ones.

You get a lot of them that are overrated. They're not good. They think they are. They get good stories, because the newspapers get buffaloed. But they're not good.

But I know the negotiators in the world, and I put them one for each country. Believe me, folks. We will do very, very well, very, very well.

But I wouldn't even waste my time with this one. I would call up the head of Ford, who I know. If I was president, I'd say, "Congratulations. I understand that you're building a nice $2.5 billion car factory in Mexico and that you're going to take your cars and sell them to the United States zero tax, just flow them across the border."

And you say to yourself, "How does that help us," right? "How does that help us? Where is that good"? It's not.

So I would say, "Congratulations. That's the good news. Let me give you the bad news. Every car and every truck and every part manufactured in this plant that comes across the border, we're going to charge you a 35-percent tax, and that tax is going to be paid simultaneously with the transaction, and that's it.

Now, here's what is going to happen. If it's not me in the position, it's one of these politicians that we're running against, you know, the 400 people that we're (inaudible). And here's what's going to happen. They're not so stupid. They know it's not a good thing, and they may even be upset by it. But then they're going to get a call from the donors or probably from the lobbyist for Ford and say, "You can't do that to Ford, because Ford takes care of me and I take care of you, and you can't do that to Ford."

And guess what? No problem. They're going to build in Mexico. They're going to take away thousands of jobs. It's very bad for us.

So under President Trump, here's what would happen:

The head of Ford will call me back, I would say within an hour after I told them the bad news. But it could be he'd want to be cool, and he'll wait until the next day. You know, they want to be a little cool.

And he'll say, "Please, please, please." He'll beg for a little while, and I'll say, "No interest." Then he'll call all sorts of political people, and I'll say, "Sorry, fellas. No interest," because I don't need anybody's money. It's nice. I don't need anybody's money.

I'm using my own money. I'm not using the lobbyists. I'm not using donors. I don't care. I'm really rich. I (inaudible).

And by the way, I'm not even saying that's the kind of mindset, that's the kind of thinking you need for this country.

So— because we got to make the country rich.

It sounds crass. Somebody said, "Oh, that's crass." It's not crass.

We got $18 trillion in debt. We got nothing but problems.

We got a military that needs equipment all over the place. We got nuclear weapons that are obsolete.

We've got nothing. We've got Social Security that's going to be destroyed if somebody like me doesn't bring money into the country. All these other people want to cut the hell out of it. I'm not going to cut it at all; I'm going to bring money in, and we're going to save it.

But here's what's going to happen:

After I'm called by 30 friends of mine who contributed to different campaigns, after I'm called by all of the special interests and by the— the donors and by the lobbyists— and they have zero chance at convincing me, zero— I'll get a call the next day from the head of Ford. He'll say. "Please reconsider," I'll say no.

He'll say, "Mr. President, we've decided to move the plant back to the United States, and we're not going to build it in Mexico." That's it. They have no choice. They have no choice.

There are hundreds of things like that. I'll give you another example.

Saudi Arabia, they make $1 billion a day. One billion dollars a day. I love the Saudis. Many are in this building. They make a billion dollars a day. Whenever they have problems, we send over the ships. We say "we're gonna protect." What are we doing? They've got nothing but money.

If the right person asked them, they'd pay a fortune. They wouldn't be there except for us.

And believe me, you look at the border with Yemen. You remember Obama a year ago, Yemen was a great victory. Two weeks later, the place was blown up. Everybody got out— and they kept our equipment.

They always keep our equipment. We ought to send used equipment, right? They always keep our equipment. We ought to send some real junk, because, frankly, it would be— we ought to send our surplus. We're always losing this gorgeous brand-new stuff.

But look at that border with Saudi Arabia. Do you really think that these people are interested in Yemen? Saudi Arabia without us is gone. They're gone.

And I'm the one that made all of the right predictions about Iraq. You know, all of these politicians that I'm running against now— it's so nice to say I'm running as opposed to if I run, if I run. I'm running.

But all of these politicians that I'm running against now, they're trying to disassociate. I mean, you looked at Bush, it took him five days to answer the question on Iraq. He couldn't answer the question. He didn't know. I said, "Is he intelligent?"

Then I looked at Rubio. He was unable to answer the question, is Iraq a good thing or bad thing? He didn't know. He couldn't answer the question.

How are these people gonna lead us? How are we gonna — how are we gonna go back and make it great again? We can't. They don't have a clue. They can't lead us. They can't. They can't even answer simple questions. It was terrible.

But Saudi Arabia is in big, big trouble. Now, thanks to fracking and other things, the oil is all over the place. And I used to say it, there are ships at sea, and this was during the worst crisis, that were loaded up with oil, and the cartel kept the price up, because, again, they were smarter than our leaders. They were smarter than our leaders.

There is so much wealth out there that can make our country so rich again, and therefore make it great again. Because we need money. We're dying. We're dying. We need money. We have to do it. And we need the right people.

So Ford will come back. They'll all come back. And I will say this, this is going to be an election, in my opinion, that's based on competence.

Somebody said — thank you, darlin'.

Somebody said to me the other day, a reporter, a very nice reporter, "But, Mr. Trump, you're not a nice person."

That's true. But actually I am. I think I am a nice person. People that know me, like me. Does my family like me? I think so, right. Look at my family. I'm proud of my family.

By the way, speaking of my family, Melania, Barron, Kai, Donnie, Don, Vanessa, Tiffany, Ivanka did a great job. Did she do a great job?

Great. Jared, Laura and Eric, I'm very proud of my family. They're a great family.

So the reporter said to me the other day, "But, Mr. Trump, you're not a nice person. How can you get people to vote for you?"

I said, "I don't know." I said, "I think that number one, I am a nice person. I give a lot of money away to charities and other things. I think I'm actually a very nice person."

But, I said, "This is going to be an election that's based on competence, because people are tired of these nice people. And they're tired of being ripped off by everybody in the world. And they're tired of spending more money on education than any nation in the world per capita, than any nation in the world, and we are 26th in the world, 25 countries are better than us in education. And some of them are like third world countries. But we're becoming a third word country, because of our infrastructure, our airports, our roads, everything. So one of the things I did, and I said, you know what I'll do. I'll do it. Because a lot of people said, "He'll never run. Number one, he won't want to give up his lifestyle."

They're right about that, but I'm doing it.

Number two, I'm a private company, so nobody knows what I'm worth. And the one thing is that when you run, you have to announce and certify to all sorts of governmental authorities your net worth.

I said, "I don't know." I said, "I think that number one, I am a nice person. I give a lot of money away to charities and other things. I think I'm actually a very nice person."

But, I said, "This is going to be an election that's based on competence, because people are tired of these nice people. And they're tired of being ripped off by everybody in the world. And they're tired of spending more money on education than any nation in the world per capita, than any nation in the world, and we are 26th in the world, 25 countries are better than us in education. And some of them are like third world countries. But we're becoming a third word country, because of our infrastructure, our airports, our roads, everything. So one of the things I did, and I said, you know what I'll do. I'll do it. Because a lot of people said, "He'll never run. Number one, he won't want to give up his lifestyle."

They're right about that, but I'm doing it.

Number two, I'm a private company, so nobody knows what I'm worth. And the one thing is that when you run, you have to announce and certify to all sorts of governmental authorities your net worth.

So I said, "That's OK." I'm proud of my net worth. I've done an amazing job.

I started off— thank you— I started off in a small office with my father in Brooklyn and Queens, and my father said — and I love my father. I learned so much. He was a great negotiator. I learned so much just sitting at his feet playing with blocks listening to him negotiate with subcontractors. But I learned a lot.

But he used to say, "Donald, don't go into Manhattan. That's the big leagues. We don't know anything about that. Don't do it."

I said, "I gotta go into Manhattan. I gotta build those big buildings. I gotta do it, Dad. I've gotta do it."

And after four or five years in Brooklyn, I ventured into Manhattan and did a lot of great deals— the Grand Hyatt Hotel. I was responsible for the convention center on the west side. I did a lot of great deals, and I did them early and young. And now I'm building all over the world, and I love what I'm doing.

But they all said, a lot of the pundits on television, "Well, Donald will never run, and one of the main reasons is he's private and he's probably not as successful as everybody thinks."

So I said to myself, you know, nobody's ever going to know unless I run, because I'm really proud of my success. I really am.

I've employed— I've employed tens of thousands of people over my lifetime. That means medical. That means education. That means everything.

So a large accounting firm and my accountants have been working for months, because it's big and complex, and they've put together a statement, a financial statement, just a summary. But everything will be filed eventually with the government, and we don't [use] extensions or anything. We'll be filing it right on time. We don't need anything.

And it was even reported incorrectly yesterday, because they said, "He had assets of $9 billion." So I said, "No, that's the wrong number. That's the wrong number. Not assets."

So they put together this. And before I say it, I have to say this. I made it the old-fashioned way. It's real estate. You know, it's real estate.

It's labor, and it's unions good and some bad and lots of people that aren't in unions, and it's all over the place and building all over the world.

And I have assets— big accounting firm, one of the most highly respected— 9 billion 240 million dollars.

And I have liabilities of about $500 million. That's long-term debt, very low interest rates.

In fact, one of the big banks came to me and said, "Donald, you don't have enough borrowings. Could we loan you $4 billion"? I said, "I don't need it. I don't want it. And I've been there. I don't want it."

But in two seconds, they give me whatever I wanted. So I have a total net worth, and now with the increase, it'll be well-over $10 billion. But here, a total net worth of—net worth, not assets, not— a net worth, after all debt, after all expenses, the greatest assets— Trump Tower, 1290 Avenue of the Americas, Bank of America building in San Francisco, 40 Wall Street, sometimes referred to as the Trump building right opposite the New York— many other places all over the world.

So the total is $8,737,540,00.

Now I'm not doing that…

I'm not doing that to brag, because you know what? I don't have to brag. I don't have to, believe it or not.

I'm doing that to say that that's the kind of thinking our country needs. We need that thinking. We have the opposite thinking.

We have losers. We have losers. We have people that don't have it. We have people that are morally corrupt. We have people that are selling this country down the drain.

So I put together this statement, and the only reason I'm telling you about it today is because we really do have to get going, because if we have another three or four years— you know, we're at $8 trillion now. We're soon going to be at $20 trillion.

According to the economists— who I'm not big believers in, but, nevertheless, this is what they're saying— that $24 trillion— we're very close— that's the point of no return. Twenty four trillion dollars. We will be there soon. That's when we become Greece. That's when we become a country that's unsalvageable. And we're gonna be there very soon. We're gonna be there very soon.

So, just to sum up, I would do various things very quickly. I would repeal and replace the big lie, Obamacare.

I would build a great wall, and nobody builds walls better than me, believe me, and I'll build them very inexpensively, I will build a great, great wall on our southern border. And I will have Mexico pay for that wall.

Mark my words.

Nobody would be tougher on ISIS than Donald Trump. Nobody.

I will find — within our military, I will find the General Patton or I will find General MacArthur, I will find the right guy. I will find the guy that's going to take that military and make it really work. Nobody, nobody will be pushing us around.

I will stop Iran from getting nuclear weapons. And we won't be using a man like Secretary Kerry that has absolutely no concept of negotiation, who's making a horrible and laughable deal, who's just being tapped along as they make weapons right now, and then goes into a bicycle race at 72 years old, and falls and breaks his leg. I won't be doing that. And I promise I will never be in a bicycle race. That I can tell you.

I will immediately terminate President Obama's illegal executive order on immigration, immediately.

Fully support and back up the Second Amendment.

Now, it's very interesting. Today I heard it. Through stupidity, in a very, very hard core prison, interestingly named Clinton, two vicious murderers, two vicious people escaped, and nobody knows where they are. And a woman was on television this morning, and she said, "You know, Mr. Trump," and she was telling other people, and I actually called her, and she said, "You know, Mr. Trump, I always was against guns. I didn't want guns. And now since this happened"— it's up in the prison area— "my husband and I are finally in agreement, because he wanted the guns. We now have a gun on every table. We're ready to start shooting."

I said, "Very interesting."

So protect the Second Amendment.

End — end Common Core. Common Core should — it is a disaster. Bush is totally in favor of Common Core. I don't see how he can possibly get the nomination. He's weak on immigration. He's in favor of Common Core. How the hell can you vote for this guy? You just can't do it. We have to end education has to be local.

Rebuild the country's infrastructure.

Nobody can do that like me. Believe me. It will be done on time, on budget, way below cost, way below what anyone ever thought.

I look at the roads being built all over the country, and I say I can build those things for one-third. What they do is unbelievable, how bad.

You know, we're building on Pennsylvania Avenue, the Old Post Office, we're converting it into one of the world's great hotels. It's gonna be the best hotel in Washington, D.C. We got it from the General Services Administration in Washington. The Obama administration. We got it. It was the most highly sought after — or one of them, but I think the most highly sought after project in the history of General Services. We got it. People were shocked, Trump got it.

Well, I got it for two reasons. Number one, we're really good. Number two, we had a really good plan. And I'll add in the third, we had a great financial statement. Because the General Services, who are terrific people, by the way, and talented people, they wanted to do a great job. And they wanted to make sure it got built.

So we have to rebuild our infrastructure, our bridges, our roadways, our airports. You come into La Guardia Airport, it's like we're in a third world country. You look at the patches and the 40-year-old floor. They throw down asphalt, and they throw.

You look at these airports, we are like a third world country. And I come in from China and I come in from Qatar and I come in from different places, and they have the most incredible airports in the world. You come to back to this country and you have LAX, disaster. You have all of these disastrous airports. We have to rebuild our infrastructure.

Save Medicare, Medicaid and Social Security without cuts. Have to do it.

Get rid of the fraud. Get rid of the waste and abuse, but save it. People have been paying it for years. And now many of these candidates want to cut it. You save it by making the United States, by making us rich again, by taking back all of the money that's being lost.

Renegotiate our foreign trade deals.

Reduce our $18 trillion in debt, because, believe me, we're in a bubble. We have artificially low interest rates. We have a stock market that, frankly, has been good to me, but I still hate to see what's happening. We have a stock market that is so bloated.

Be careful of a bubble because what you've seen in the past might be small potatoes compared to what happens. So be very, very careful.

And strengthen our military and take care of our vets. So, so important.

Sadly, the American dream is dead.

But if I get elected president I will bring it back bigger and better and stronger than ever before, and we will make America great again.

Thank you. Thank you very much.

--

Altogether, Trump will give America a fighting chance to be the best it can be. He's strong, willing and a proud American. His policies will put Americans first – and many of his plans will directly provide benefits to black Americans in quest of safety, prosperity and improved quality of life.

www.ingramcontent.com/pod-product-compliance
Lightning Source LLC
Chambersburg PA
CBHW071158280526
45787CB00002B/541